A WOMAN UNCHAINED

Breaking the silence of childhood sexual abuse.
A Warrior's Journey!

A WOMAN UNCHAINED

Breaking the silence of childhood sexual abuse.
A Warrior's Journey!

Written by

Sherika Powell

MERAKI HOUSE
P U B L I S H I N G

(C) 2016 by Sherika Powell

Published by **MERAKI HOUSE PUBLISHING INC.**

For any information regarding permission contact
Sherika Powell via

info@sherikapowell.com

Printed in the United States of America
First publication, 2016.

Paperback ISBN 978-1-988364-06-3

eBook ISBN – 978-1-988364-05-6

Book cover design by
www.designisreborn.com

Dedication

This book is dedicated to my rock: my husband *Christopher Powell* who has supported me on this journey. I am thankful every day for our soul connection. To my sons *Jacob and Christopher* and to my stepson *Tavon*, I hope through this book you will see what it means to persevere even when all the odds are against you.

Acknowledgements

First, I want to acknowledge my Lord and savior *Jesus Christ* for bringing me through this journey because without him carrying me to the place I am today, none of this would be possible.

I also want to thank my wonderful Grandmother *Ianthie Francis:* you are everything I want to be, I admire you, you have never left my side since birth, and you have always been a positive force in my life. When I felt like I had no one in my corner you showed up, you stepped in, and you loved me and supported me through everything. You always have an encouraging word for me to hear; you love the lord and you are beyond blessed.

When I think back on how you showed up for me, I am grateful. I am grateful that God appointed you to be my Grandmother. God knew I would need you to move my way through life; he knew I would need your unconditional support. Because you are the blessed person that you are, I have received numerous donations from your friends that have given graciously to make this book happen and become published.

I want to thank those angels out there that gave to my cause when they didn't even know me. I want to thank: *Bonnie Bonaventura, Pearl Dookie, Dorett Weir, Emmanuel J. Dick, Cynthia V.*

Lawson-Lurch, Trevor Graham, Raymond Conyette, Esmie Hutchinson, Iris Clark, Henry Francis, Mr. and Mrs. Hugh Spencer, Grace Neita, Janet King, Carolyn Gunter-Smith, Rema Thompson, Mary Mcdonald, Pauline Wisdom-Gillian, Hollie and Adrienne Copeland, Camelia Boyd, Lisa Windflower, Whitman Solomon, Hyacinth Taylor, Lona Freemanple, and Franca Gismondi.

I also want to thank my amazing family that has supported me through the years. To my amazing husband *Christopher,* thank you for listening to my 101 ideas and for being so supportive about my projects. You are one of a kind; I know we are a God union, and with you by my side, I know I can accomplish anything. I love you beyond words. You make me want to be a better human. I love the life we have built. Rome wasn't built in a day, but I believe with God's hand over our family we can achieve anything.

To my sons *Jacob and Christopher*, you boys are my everything. You are a part of my journey and I hope that one day you will be proud of your mommy and her will to persevere.

I want to acknowledge my sister *Omega Smith*. You and I went through so much in the beginning of our lives; you have been journeying with me through everything. We have blossomed our relationship into a great friendship, and you have been so supportive during this process—I am so thankful that you are my sister. You are always there to listen to me rant, and I appreciate it immensely.

I want to thank my father *Owen Smith:* thank you for being a safe place to land when I had none. Thank you for raising two teenage daughters alone and doing the best you could. You were a great dad, and I couldn't have asked for a better father; you were my safe haven. You are the most kind, giving person that I know; you are a blessed being in every way. Without you, I don't know where I would have ended up; thank you for being the kind of man you are.

I want to acknowledge my mother *Rashida Siddeeq.* Although I did not have you as the mother I needed when I was younger, I have you as a mother now. I see how much you have grown over the years and how far you have come on your own journey, and I know for you the best is yet to come! I appreciate your presence in my life and your full support of my book; you always encouraged me to keep pursuing my dreams.

I also want to thank my aunt *Maxine Francis.* I have always looked up to you. You were the cool aunt when I was growing up, and I so admire your words of wisdom. You were always there when I needed to talk to someone, and you never passed judgment; thank you for your support.

I also want to thank my sister-in-law *Patricia Thomas:* thank you for being so supportive over the years.

To my favorite cousin *Nicole Ramos:* thank you for all the years of support and sisterly love.

I want to thank my amazing group of girlfriends: I love you guys; you are my sisters from another mother. I appreciate your presence in my life every day. You ladies have been with me from the tough seasons of my life to the joyous ones. I appreciate our friendship beyond words. You all have motivated me and pushed me to think beyond what I can see and go for it—thank you guys for being my light. We may not see each other or communicate all the time, but I know when it counts you guys are there. Thank you, *Marisa Bacchus, Shelly Ann Rodney, Sherie Rouleau, Heather Wilson-Phillips, Angela Anderson, Neikeisha Gordon, Belinda Brammah, Nicole Wright, Bettyna Beauchamp, Latoya Samuels, and Yasheia Wilson.*

A special mention to my beloved friend *Monique Hanna* (RIP) who lost her life to domestic violence in 2015. I know you are an angel looking down on me, and you are celebrating this victory with me. I love you, girl, and I miss you terribly.

Thank you to all the supporters who donated on *GoFundMe, Mandy Oake, S. Lin, Nadine Wilson*, and *Mikeisha Paul*

Contents

Foreword

by Nicole Bromley

I believe childhood sexual abuse is one of the best-kept secrets in our world today. And, I believe that the key to healing is in survivors finding their voice. But, that is no easy mission. The shame and silence surrounding a childhood full of memories of sexual abuse can make the journey ahead seem so dark, deep, and scary that you feel you may never get out alive.

It takes courage to survive childhood trauma, and it takes even more courage to keep going after it has ended. The effects of abuse are innumerable and they last a lifetime, causing many survivors to seek unhealthy ways to numb the pain and loneliness they feel or to give up all together.

As a sexual abuse survivor myself, I understand the silent shame and masked hurt associated with childhood sexual abuse. I held my secret in for many years until I realized that the silence had to be broken for my healing to begin. Finding the courage to tell my secret released me from the shame of my past so I could embrace the future; it put me on a journey of healing where I discovered the freedom I'd been longing for. My courage to break my silence has since ignited the same courage in others. But, I know that there are still so many silent ones out there who are still searching and longing for this freedom. Sherika knows this too, and she has graciously offered us her strength and powerful testimony that will assuredly spark healing for all who read her story.

I can remember what it was like to feel alone, and, furthermore, I recall what reading the stories of others did to help heal that void—not only hearing about those who have experienced similar trauma, but hearing of their triumphs as well. Inspiring testimonies help us keep moving on this lifelong healing journey when we feel like giving up. Real life stories remind us that real hope is still alive today and that it's always within reach. Sherika's story is a testimony of strength, of hope, and of survival at all costs.

In a world full of bad news, pain, and fear, we must be reminded of stories like Sherika's. We need to know we are not alone and that there are others out there who have not only survived, but who are thriving. May Sherika's life be a reminder that we are all worth the fight for truth, freedom, and wholeness. As you read, may you find hope and courage in the midst of whatever you are walking through.

Your story matters. Your voice matters. God bless your journey.

Nicole Braddock Bromley

Survivor, Author, Speaker

Founder of **www.iamonevoice.org** and **www.onevoice4freedom.org**

Introduction

Thank you for taking the opportunity to read all about my journey to A Woman Unchained! Why we journey through life the way we do can sometimes be a mystery. We often wonder where a path may take us and why we are faced with a traumatic event. I can tell you that going through life's lessons and challenges thus far on this earth have brought me to where I am today. Was the struggle real? Of course! Did I feel defeated at times? Yes! But a greater plan was in store for me. Writing this book has been a part of my life journey; I had to go through these growing pains to get to where I am today to share with all of you and be candid about the struggles I faced and the heartache I endured. Not only is this a story about facing tough life experiences and challenges, but it is also a story of hope, love, and faith. It is a journey about how to activate your faith, persevere through the tough seasons, set goals, and get on with living your best life!

Through A Woman Unchained I hope you get inspired about your life, and about what you can do if you just believe in yourself a little more than you did yesterday. If you just decide that today, this very day, you are going to make some bold moves and some positive changes, you will be closer to a purposeful life. Statistics Canada states that one in three girls are sexually assaulted by the time they turn 18. Although I am part of this group and share the same statistic with so many others, I have chosen not to be a victim of my circumstance, but a survivor. I hope through sharing my experiences, struggles, and triumphs, I will be a beacon of light to those that have lost hope and feel like they will forever carry this heavy burden and label: a victim of sexual abuse.

I am here to say there is light at the end of the tunnel. There is joy, and I have found peace, comfort and healing in God's love for me. Despite all the difficult obstacles and barriers that were against me as a child, I still rose from the ashes and persevered. Being a survivor of childhood sexual abuse does something to a person; it leaves you with scars so deep that often manifest into feelings of low self-worth and shame. I experienced all of that—and then some.

It is crucial to educate our children from an early age about awareness of themselves their bodies and what is appropriate touch and what is not. It is important that we give our children the free space to say what they feel and not to be afraid of the consequences like I was. In order to keep our children safe from predators, our conversations with them in my opinion need to begin as early as four years old. The statistics on how many children are affected by sexual abuse are staggering—and they don't seem to be improving.

In 2005, Canadian statistics had the rate of sexual assault against children and youth at over five times higher than for adults—206 children and youth victims compared to 39 adult victims for every 100,000 people.

The overall worldwide statistics state that over 40 million children are subjected to abuse each year.

Cited: (Found on Department of Justice Canada Website (article titled: Sexual Abuse and Exploitation of Children and Youth: A Fact Sheet from the Department of Justice Canada)

http://www.justice.gc.ca/eng/rp-pr/cp-pm/cr-rc/dig/prot.html

www.arkofhopeforchildren.org http://arkofhopeforchildren.org/child-abuse/child-abuse-statistics-info

These statistics are alarming and frightening. As a community we must do our part in protecting our children as best as we can. As a society, we can contribute to the prevention of child abuse by breaking the silence and speaking out even when it is difficult to do so. It is going to take a village to end this epidemic. This is my coming out story. No longer am I ashamed of my past, but I look forward to a bright tomorrow. My chains are gone, and I have been set free! The silent child is no more but now...*A Woman Unchained!*

Chapter 1

MY PAST DOES NOT DEFINE MY FUTURE

"When you go through deep waters I will be with you"

~ Isaiah 43:2

I was born October 15, 1982 to a single mother, at the time and one sibling, my big sister Omega. My parents broke up around the time I was born. I grew up in Toronto, Canada, generally a well-adjusted, happy child. I enjoyed playing outside, playing with my sister, and just being a kid. When I was around eight years old, my mother married my stepfather from Jamaica. Shortly after they married, he came to Canada to live with us. We were one big happy blended family. My sister and I still visited our biological dad on the weekends, which we always looked forward to as our dad was our hero. He would always have some fun outings for us to go on, whether it be an amusement park or day trips: it was never a dull moment. I felt loved by my dad and fortunate that he was in my life. My sister and I were his little princesses.

As time went on, I became well-adjusted to my new stepfather as he always made time for me to teach me new things and take me on outings to the park; we even took a karate class together. I considered myself lucky to not only have my dad, but to also have a stepfather who cared for us. Our family grew over the years with two baby sisters and a stepsister (from my stepfather's previous relationship) from Jamaica.

Things were drastically changing with new extensions to the family and my dad moving to Florida a few years later. During that time, we began to practice Islam, leaving Christianity behind. That's when, for me, the dynamics drastically changed in our family and went downhill. Prior to my mother getting married my sister and I would attend Sunday school and church. By the age of nine, I no longer attended church. We were introduced to a new religion Islam. I had to wear a hijab to school and attend madrasa class at the mosque to learn more about Islam. At that time I felt like my world was turned upside down. I did not adjust well. This new religion was foreign to me and confusing. As that young girl I wondered why we had to change, what was wrong with the old one? As we were Christians prior to Islam. I felt like I was being torn between two worlds and I didn't understand why we had to change as none of this was explained to me. Although I didn't understand what was really transpiring in our family I had no choice but to oblige.

Our once-happy, blended family was slowly deteriorating. My childhood was no longer a happy one. The thought of coming home after school was dreadful. I hated coming home; I just wanted to stay at school for as long as possible to avoid the controlling atmosphere that was waiting for me. When I was home, I buried my nose in a book to get away from my reality. Books were my escape; I would spend countless hours reading or going to the library—that was my safe place. As the dynamic in our home was rapidly changing, adding new family members and our new religion, so was the relationship with my stepfather as he was becoming more and more controlling over our lives.

Although my stepfather became even more controlling over the household, he was still interested in taking me out on day trips, to the park, out for ice cream even occasionally just giving me a hug to showed he cared. One day, the hugs became uncomfortable. They started to last a little too long and feelings of awkwardness began to creep in. Then the touching began. I was around nine years old when I knew I was being inappropriately touched. I'll never forget that feeling.

As a child, I didn't know what to call it or if I should tell anyone, but I knew that it felt wrong. It would happen occasionally—the inappropriate hugging periods as I knew them—and then it eventually stopped. I decided to keep it to myself as I didn't have a name for it and didn't understand what was happening, other than feeling uncomfortable.

While I continued to try to make sense of what was happening to me, something horrific was about to happen to my sister.

One day, I came home to find my sister sitting on the dining table looking slumped over and upset. My mom was scolding her, and I found out quickly she had been caught stealing. From what I could gather, as a form of punishment, my mother gave my stepfather permission to punish her. So my sister was beaten, lash after lash after lash. I waited and waited for it to be over and for my sister to stop screaming, but it felt like it would go on forever. My mother was also present but said nothing; she just let the beating continue. Finally, he stopped. He came out of our room that we shared, where he was beating her with his belt, and I ran to see her. My sister was beaten so badly that there were belt welts and bruises all over her body. She could barely crawl into her bed to cry herself to sleep. My heart ached for her. I felt so helpless. I thought to myself, who is this person living with us? Our stepfather is a monster.

My sister was around thirteen at the time and decided to take matters into her own hands. She called the police, very shortly after the incident, to report the beating. Since the physical evidence on my sister made it clear that she had been abused, our stepfather was arrested for assault and taken out of our home in handcuffs. My sister and I did not go back home that night; we spent a few nights in foster care until we were taken in by my grandmother and my aunts.

At the ages of thirteen and eleven, my sister and I were abused and left homeless, abandoned to be shuffled amongst family. Our mother had chosen her husband over her daughters. I remember feeling extremely sad, lonely, abandoned, and confused at that time in my life—a time when I needed her most. My sister and I were motherless children, physically and spiritually.

When we left foster care and stayed with relatives for a while, things became somewhat normal. We still had limited connection and communication with my mother. Her main concern was my stepfather and getting him out of jail. I felt a longing for her. Even though she abandoned us, I missed my mom. Despite all the dysfunction happening around me, she was my mom. It wasn't home. As much as I wanted to be home with my mother, I did not want to be anywhere near my stepfather. I was afraid that what happened to my sister may happen to me as well. I felt my mother had really no say in our family function, she just did what our step father wanted to do.

I didn't really grasp the concept of neglect or abandonment and the damage it had done. As a result, I felt I felt directionless for many years into my adulthood. The one person who should have been there for us during this difficult time, didn't want me or my sister.

I believed that mothers were supposed to protect you, love you, and look out for your well-being. I had neither up to that point. At that time, being so young, I didn't understand it, but my mother did not have the tools to parent my sister and me in a healthy way. I know now that she was going through her own major battles and did the best she could at the time with what she knew. This revelation did not come to me overnight as it took many years to get to that place. I was bitter for a long time with so many unanswered questions. But I know now that God was, and is, my comfort in times of turmoil. He is the same yesterday, today, and always.

Through this book, I hope you find your own inspiration and courage. Through my story, I hope you come to know that there is hope in the struggle and that through his grace, it can and will get better. Storms are temporary but his love for us is forever. As you continue to delve into the pages of my journey, I hope you are inspired to break free and become unchained from the circumstances in your life that may be holding you back from experiencing real joy. I hope that you find the courage to conquer your goliath and know that everything can be turned around for the good.

Chapter 2

THE CAGED BIRD

"There are wounds that never show on the body that are deeper and more hurtful than anything that bleeds."

~ Laurell K. Hamilton

After my stepfather's charges for assaulting my sister were dealt with, I returned home, while my sister remained with relatives. We were torn apart. Despite the obvious dysfunction of our home life, I longed for a mother that cared and loved me. I returned home hoping she was still in there somewhere. My stepfather had returned from jail and all seemed well—or as good as it was going to get at the time. I was visited by social workers to make sure that things in the home were working out for me. I told the social workers that everything was fine; I just wanted my mother back. But things were not the same without my sister—I missed her terribly. And I didn't know it yet, but I was about to miss her a whole lot more.

As I finished grade six in Toronto, my mom, stepfather, my younger sisters, and I packed what little belongings we had and moved to Florida. My mother had gotten a job as a nurse there. It was bittersweet; although I was excited to be living in a sunny place I was going to miss my family. We had left all of my extended family, relatives, and my sister behind in Canada.

Florida was beautiful—great weather and beautiful beaches, but it would never be home. I enrolled in middle school, which was not easy for me to get used to as everything seemed so different at an American school, but I managed. It was a big transition for me, and I mostly kept to myself. I was often bullied for being the only Canadian person literally in the school and for speaking without an American accent which the other kids thought was weird. So literally every time I opened my mouth in class there seemed to be always some mocking from other students in the background. That led me to shut down and keep quiet. I was also teased about my looks relentlessly, which also made it hard for me to feel comfortable.

I was often called ugly on numerous occasions which deflated my self-esteem and my home life certainly solidified that claim. I spent most of my time indoors either watching my younger sisters or burying my nose in a book. I felt very alone and alienated from the world. We would spend a lot of time at the local mosque praying and participating in mosque activities. My mother and stepfather were very active in the Islam faith. I recall often the vague memories of my mother sending us to Sunday school. I often wondered what had happened to those beliefs I had about Jesus.

Little did I know, many years later, all would be revealed to me, including how the power, love, and grace of God sustained me all these years.

During this time, I slowly began feeling safe again. I started making new friends and integrating myself into school. My relationship with my mother was going well and I was beginning to feel like I had my mother back. One weekend, my mom had to go out of town for business. I did not recall the specifics of the business trip, but I knew she would be away for the weekend, which meant that I was left alone with my sisters and stepfather. I did not think anything of it as things had been going well with my stepfather. So when my mom left for the weekend, I proceeded with my weekend chores.

We lived in an apartment so I had to take the laundry downstairs for washing. As I went downstairs and entered the laundry room I saw this boy that rode the same bus to school with me. He lived in the same apartment building as me and was extremely abrasive and creepy. He was always saying inappropriate things to me about my body that I did not like. He would always follow me into the staircase at school and try to force himself on me.

This happened a few times, but I was too ashamed to say anything for I felt I would get blamed. I managed to fight him off every time, and he finally left me alone. But this time, I was cornered. He came into the laundry room and began trying to force himself on me. I fought back but not enough. He managed to pin me to the ground. He was winning, and I started to panic; with his weight, on me I couldn't move. Suddenly, I heard a yell, a voice that sounded like my stepfather. It was my stepfather, and he raced in and snatched the boy off me with one yank. I was so relieved. I was saved! I was so glad that he came to my rescue.

That thought lasted for about two minutes until I realized he was not on my side at all. I was scolded and slapped repeatedly for leading the boy on, and I was told it was my fault. I was so confused. How is it that I was so close to being sexually assaulted, yet I was the one at fault? I was being reprimanded for it as if I had caused it in some way? I didn't understand. All I could feel was a great deal of shame as I tried to understand how I was at fault.

My stepfather and I went upstairs back to the apartment and that was where my hell began. My stepfather was extremely angry with me. He repeatedly slapped me over and over, calling me names. The level of confusion was beyond me. I just didn't understand why this was happening. I wondered why he wasn't helping me. Finally, he ordered me to the bathroom saying that he needed to see if I was still a virgin. I didn't understand what he meant. What was a virgin? So, I did as he said. I took off my bottoms and underwear, and he did something to me I didn't understand at that time. It was only later, after the shock and confusion subsided, that I realized I was raped by my stepfather that night.

I couldn't believe what had happened. Had it really happened? According to my stepfather, it had but was my fault. Again. He told me I was to feel ashamed for what had happened and that I had brought it on myself. He warned me not to tell my mother because it was all my doing, all my fault. I felt like I had escaped one traumatic experience only to be in another. But, I obeyed. I didn't dare tell my mother. I felt the shame my stepfather had insisted I should have, and confused as to why it had happened to me in the first place.

When my mother returned from her trip, I acted like my old self. I tried to act like nothing had happened. Even though I said nothing, she seemed upset with me. Deep down I knew he had told her some sort of story about the events that took place, but somehow whatever story he had told her it was my fault too. She scolded me for the story my stepfather had told her something about the situation I had been found in with the boy in my building. Once again, another layer of shame and guilt that I was to carry with nowhere to turn, no one who would listen, and no one who would ever believe me. My mother, in her rage, began to beat me and call me names. This was my punishment for apparently leading on the boy or whatever story my stepfather had told my mother.

As I look back now, I can't help but remember the confusion I felt. I was girl in middle school, who in the space of 48 hours had been assaulted, shamed, raped, and completely stripped of my dignity and my self-worth—sexually abused, physically abused, and emotionally abused. It was like the world stood still. Suddenly, I felt like no one was on my side, not even God. I wondered if there was even a God anyway… Surely not.

Although as a family we were practicing Muslims, I had checked out of all religion and God. I believed in nothing. My stepfather never spoke of the incident nor did any other abuse situations come up after that. I was never inclined to tell my mother the truth because, based on her actions, I knew she wouldn't believe me. My stepfather did a very good job of painting the scenario in his favor and manipulating my mother to believe his version of what happened. So much so, I was now the untrustworthy daughter in my mother's eyes. I was to be blamed and shamed.

I began to retreat from life. I started to spend more time alone and stuck to myself at school. I missed my home back in Canada, my family, and I missed my sister more than ever. If only she were here, she would understand. She would have kept me safe.

From then on, I did what I knew would take my mind off what had happened: reading books. I just read and read all the time. This was my coping mechanism; it helped me escape from my home life which I didn't know was about to get a whole lot worse.

I had completed grade seven in Miami, Florida. It was one of the most difficult years, but I got through it. My mother had gotten a new job in southern Florida, so we decided to move, which meant changing schools again. I was entering grade eight that fall. In our home it was strongly enforced that I wear the hijab to school. I had no interest in Islam or any other religion and wanted nothing more than to just fit in and feel some sort of sense of being "normal." So, sometimes I didn't wear it. I was reprimanded quite often when I didn't wear the hijab, but I really didn't care. I just stuffed it in my backpack as I left the house each morning, and resumed wearing it when I returned home. As the days and weeks went by, I lived in isolation. I wasn't allowed to go out with friends or have any friends over. It was school, home and the mosque that was it. I often stood on our balcony watching people go by, fantasizing about what it was like to be them: to feel free. I felt like a caged bird.

I felt extreme sadness. I wanted to be a normal kid: laugh, have friends over, go on outings just be like everyone else. But, this cage was my reality. So, as time went by, I continued to watch from my balcony as others lived their lives. I just watched and waited, waited for the day I'd be set free.

Chapter 3

Broken but Not Forgotten

"God can restore what is broken and change it into something amazing. All you need is Faith."

~ Joel 2:25

Living in the house was getting to be quite difficult for me as I felt like I was always being controlled by my stepfather, and he manipulated my mother quite easily. I had not been abused for a while, and I tried very hard to suppress the memories of the end of my innocence as well as my fading childhood. Unfortunately, my memories of that horrific night would be coming back to haunt me. I was now going into grade eight, and I was looking forward to connecting with new kids at my school. The beginning of the school year began with some optimism. However, my home life would never be the same. My stepfather had begun to make comments about my body that made me very uncomfortable. My mother began working nights, which meant I was often home alone with my stepfather. One night after my mother went on her night shift, I was called into their bedroom by my stepfather.

That night, my worst nightmare came back to haunt me. I

was raped, again. At the time I didn't really have a full understanding of what sex was or that what we were doing was even sex. I was a confused little girl, slowly losing a piece of her soul every time her innocence was taken. When he was finished, he told me not to say anything—to keep this a secret—and so I did. I kept it all bottled up inside. Who'd believe me anyway? My stepfather had my mother convinced that I was the one at fault for everything. He did a very good job of making sure my mother thought I was a liar and I could not be trusted.

My grades began to slip at school as I became consumed by my home life. I could no longer focus at school or concentrate on anything. I was often tired and struggled to stay awake in class. I spent my nights lying awake, waiting for him to come into my bedroom. This went on for quite some time. All the while, I was being trained to stay quiet and put a smile on my face.

My life, looking back, was like living in a controlled, alienating environment; I felt like less than a human being most of time. I prayed to God (although I didn't have much faith in his abilities at the time), begging that if he was real, he would get me out of this hell. I didn't know that prayer would be answered very soon.

School had let out for the summer so that meant more time at home. I spent most of my summer indoors and babysitting my little sisters; I couldn't wait to go back to school. The sexual abuse had stopped for a while, and I was relieved, but it soon started up again. This time my stepfather decided to take me out to show me Miami. At first, I thought that was nice since I didn't get out much; I quickly learned the truth, that he had other plans for me. One time, he decided to rape me in the family van instead of the house. I still did not understand why this was happening to me. I did not understand why I deserved to be abused, repeatedly. One thing I was sure of was that it must be my fault. I must have been doing something to make my stepfather treat me this way. I convinced myself it was all my fault.

The night that changed my faith was when he finally got caught. One night, he had decided to take me out in the evening for a drive. He admitted to me that he needed to stop what he was doing and stated that he actually wanted to stop. He said that tonight would be the last night. I thought to myself, *"Finally! My pain will be over; this is the last time!"* Funny enough, whether he meant it or not, it was his last time because he got caught this time. While we were in the van outside the house again, I heard police sirens. Finally, I was going to be rescued! Police banged on the van and told us to get out, and the next thing I knew, he was being rushed into the back of a police cruiser. A female officer had taken me aside, and she was trying to console me. She asked me many questions about what had just occurred. I was feeling relieved that finally someone was on my side—someone was going to help me.

She called my mother at work and told her what had occurred, and my mother rushed home once she was informed. The rest of that night is a blur, but I remember feeling so relieved to know that this monster would finally be out of our lives and we could move on. Or, so I thought. My mother was devastated at the time; she truly had no idea this was happening under her own roof. For her, she felt betrayed, and I'm sure she was in a state of disbelief for the most part. We were assigned prosecutors to assist with my case. I had to make a verbal and written account for every sexual assault.

It was very draining, being asked the same thing over and over, and I was exhausted. We followed all the procedures that were asked of us. They took me to the hospital to be examined by a doctor; which I was later told to gather evidence. My mom seemed like she was very supportive, consoling me, and letting me know that everything was going to be OK. My stepfather was finally away from me, and I was away from my living hell.

My mom and I ended up in court when the judge decided to hand him his sentence—I guess we had to be there. I can remember the sentence ruling as if it were yesterday. He was released into my mother's care and ordered to mandatory counselling. No substantial jail sentence. No ruling for him to be locked away like I had hoped. I don't know how that happened, but it did. The court system had failed me. I was devastated. I truly thought my mom wanted to believe me but she could not let go of this man. She had abandoned us before for our stepfather, and this occurrence of events, unfortunately, would be no different. I felt like I meant nothing to her anymore.

Now, as an adult, I can see my mother's self-esteem and self-worth were rock bottom back then, leaving me with very little, as a child, to grab onto. I was robbed of a mother during those years; I didn't have one. I wanted her to believe me, I wanted her to wrap her arms around me and say all the rights things, and I wanted her to love me. I know now that my mother wasn't cable of loving and protecting me—she didn't even know how to love herself.

Looking back, I realize now, God brought me through all these trials and tribulations for a reason because without God holding me up back then I don't know how I would have made it. Even though I was skeptical of his existence and I was not sure he heard all of my cries, I can say today I stand firm on faith and his word that he is why I am here today.

My mother had somehow managed to convince the judges and lawyers that he wasn't a threat and that counseling would be his best option. So, no jail time for my stepfather—just probation for a short period of time. I was mortified. My mother was not in my corner, she chose her husband over me, and she continued to do so for many years to come. I was violated emotionally, physically, and spiritually. I felt broken inside. My stepfather attempted to make some heartless apology and life was just supposed to go back to the way things were before. Some sort of dysfunctional normalcy.

It never did. I was never the same. The big pink elephant in the room remained, and I was constantly uncomfortable. I was treated like a liar and an outcast in my own family, like it was still my fault. My mother took her husband's side and chose to live in denial. Things got very difficult and hostile for me in the house. The blinders were off, and I now knew I was the victim of sexual abuse. I was an angry child, and I wanted out of that house. So I rebelled in every way possible. I knew my dad moved to Florida with my sister as they had moved there recently, but I didn't know where. After many phone calls to family in Canada, I finally managed to find the information I needed to contact my dad through family in Canada by many phone calls. I was preparing to leave, to run away to my dad and my sister, but I just didn't know when or how.

The last night in that house is vague to me, but I do remember my mother yelling that she was going kick me out of the house, hitting and punching me, she wanted me gone. So I packed all I had, and my mother and stepfather dropped me off in the middle of the night at my dad's doorstep. I was once again unwanted by my mother; she left me and didn't bother to turn back. Before she dropped me off, she warned me to never tell my dad what had happened. And, I never did.

As my dad opened the door, he was very startled and taken aback; how did I show up at his doorstep in the middle of the night? I stayed with my dad and my sister from that point on. My dad still had no clue about all the issues in that home, and I didn't tell him my story until many years later. So from then on, I was living with my dad and sister. I was relieved to be out of that house with my stepfather and mother. I was finally free! My prayers were answered, restoring my faith that everything was going to work out for the good.

Life with my dad and my sister was great. It took some time to adjust, but it worked out wonderfully. It was so different but I felt a lot more comfortable in dad's house. My sister and I were finally reunited, but that didn't come without its trials and tribulations. My sister was used to being the only child in the home until I showed up, which I felt was hard for her to adjust to. But, we managed. My relationship with my sister had many ups and downs, but no matter what, I felt glad to just be around her after the long separation. I enrolled in the same high school as my sister, and, in my mind, I erased all the memories of my abusive past and stuffed them down deep where no one could find them, not even myself.

Unlike my earlier years, my high school years were vibrant, fun, and exciting. I had a good group of friends, and I was doing pretty well in my classes. I had nothing to complain about; life was good. I was a normal teenager with normal teenage issues, finally. My dad was, and will always be, my rock. He did the best he could with my sister and I, and I couldn't have asked for anything more. He gave us a good home, love, and care. During those times I had limited contact with my mother and that didn't bother me one bit. My sister went on her own to see my mom, but I never joined for a long time, I wasn't ready. My mother had treated me like the dirt under her shoe. I was not interested in being around her. I felt at the time that if I were dead she would have rejoiced. Since she moved mountains and water to be with her husband, I just figured it didn't matter much if I was dead or alive. I still had a lot of bitterness and anger towards her. In my world, she was dead to me. It was the only way I could cope with how she had treated me.

Years passed, my sister graduated high school and moved back to Canada to pursue post-secondary school. I was left alone, not entirely though as I had a new baby brother who I adored. My mother and I tried to rekindle some normalcy as she would take me on weekends to spend time with my little sisters. We never talked about the abuse or how she treated me, we just existed under false pretenses. We shoved everything under the rug and pretended as if nothing had transpired. My mother was no longer with her husband but not by her choice. I had found out that he was in jail. I wasn't sure of the circumstances. All I knew was that he was there. She continued to support him while he was in jail. In the back of my mind, I knew this relationship we were having was only temporary and that she would go back to him if she could.

The year 2000 was the year I graduated, and I surrounded myself with good friends and the love of my father. I graduated from high school, and I knew my time in Florida would be up. By the end of the summer, I was going back to Canada to live and attend post-secondary school just as my sister had done. I was excited. I missed Canada; it was always my home.

Over the years, my dad and I grew very close. I believe my dad and I are kindred spirits: we are so much alike in so many ways yet also different. He was my constant rock back then; he kept me safe and grounded. He wasn't perfect by any means, but he gave the very best of what he had to make us feel loved. And for that, my dad will always be my star. I thank God for a father like that.

It was time for me to go back to Canada and leave Florida, the second home I had come to know for many years. My dad had a hard time with it at first and so did I, yet I still held on to my secret. My coping mechanisms had worked. They had carried me through all of my teenage years into young adulthood. My coping mechanisms were 1) avoid 2) block out. That is how I survived—or so I thought—not knowing all along that it was the Holy Spirit carrying me through those trying times and through God's grace I landed into adulthood. I developed a tough Teflon-like exterior. I didn't let anyone near me on an intimate level for a long time. I was the no-nonsense girl that was quick to dismiss anyone.

I had no tolerance for others that didn't fit my views or my way of thinking. They were quickly dismissed, and I was onto the next. This included friends and family. I think throughout the years; I had created a false sense of self. I was a great actress. I had been acting and playing "the part" of a good, obedient girl since I was nine years old! I was extremely skilled at covering up things and putting on my mask. I only let others see this woman who was confident, smart, sassy, and meant "business" at all times. I fooled everyone except myself.

You see, when you are a victim of sexual abuse, often times you play these roles for protection and self-preservation—to disguise your pain, to look like you have it all together. But God knows all and sees all. You can fool man, but you can't fool him. He knows you better than you know yourself—He made you, He knows the hurt, and He knows the pain.

During this time, I was going back and forth with the decision to tell someone about what my childhood was really like. I was starting to get tired of pretending, I felt I needed to tell someone. I decided to reveal my secret to my grandmother, as I was ready to finally release my burden on someone that I trusted. They were weighing me down. I no longer wanted to keep up with the appearance like everything was OK. So, I told her what had happened in Florida; I revealed everything. No more hiding or pretending. My grandmother was shocked, upset, and devastated. But, I was relieved to finally tell someone. All those years of concealing and covering up had weighed me down.

Soon after that I told my dad too, which was extremely hard for me. My dad couldn't believe I had hidden it all those years. He said he would have never suspected a thing; it was a huge blow to him. I had acted well at that time. I could have gone years longer without anyone knowing, but I knew

I no longer wanted to carry this heavy burden around.

God gives rest to the weary, He takes our load for us, and we have no need to walk around with our head down. We are blessed and highly favored.

Once family members knew, I decided that it was time for me to begin healing. I enrolled in a short-term counseling program, which helped me get started on my self-love journey. Self-acceptance and self-love are things I had never really known before. It made sense that this was where I needed to start. So, the process began with me and my counselor. I started group counseling with survivors like myself, thinking it would be easier to disclose my past abuse that way. It was extremely helpful in opening up my eyes to the fact that I wasn't alone. So many other women were facing the same shame and hurt that I was. So many like me were trying to find healing, trying to find that place of peace.

I knew that one day I would find that inner peace, and for me through Jesus Christ, I eventually did.

I continued with the group counselling for a few short weeks, but I ended up not completing the sessions. The truth about my past and reliving it was too much to bear. I decided I could cope with out therapy and I didn't go back to counseling for almost a year.

Everyone copes with being abused differently. Some experience promiscuity, abusive relationships, mental health issues, trust issues, and the list goes on. My coping mechanism of choice was control. I wanted and needed to be in control over everything. I felt broken inside; it was terrifying going through all those horrific memories. I just wanted to forget it all and go back to the way I was coping before—wearing those masks and pretending. I found that to be much easier then dredging up the past and working through the pain. My soul was shattered into a million broken pieces. I longed for the days when I would feel whole. I wondered if I would always be this broken spirit.

Chapter 4

FROM THE VICTIM TO THE SURVIVOR

"*Hardships often prepare ordinary people for an extraordinary destiny*"

~ C.S Lewis

Since I had no control over the childhood abuse that was done to me, I decided that I would go through great lengths to control my life, my choices, and my decisions. I just thought that by acting and thinking this way I would be happier and feel a sense of calm come over my life. I made sure every decision was well documented in my calendar, which I would walk around with me everywhere. If I had left it at home, I would be on edge and anxious until I had it back in my possession. I really just thought this to be traits of a well-organized person but later found out that was not the case.

I craved control in all areas of my life and I wanted to control literally everything. If I could control when the sun rises and sundown back, then I would have! It was my drug of choice, I felt powerful. I was finding comfort in a false sense of control. I felt at the time I possessed all the power to make something out of my life. I just had to simply take control over every detail like a fine tooth come and everything would be alright. I controlled my destiny.

In those years of my life, I was far from feeling comforted by God's presence. I didn't feel God anywhere as I felt, since my childhood trauma; he was absent and left a long time ago. It was all up to me to make something out of my life: God had nothing to do with it. Looking back, God had everything to do with it. He was with me, looking out for his child even though I had denounced him.

2nd Corinthians, verse 3-4 says, *"Praise be to the God and Father of our lord Jesus Christ, the Father of compassion and the God of all comfort, who comforts us in all our troubles so that we can comfort those in any trouble with the comfort we ourselves have received from God."* Although God is ever present, back then I was struggling to find comfort in him; my soul was restless. Throughout the later years of my life I have come to know the calm that only God can give. I know now that I do not have to carry all my burdens on my own human strength, which only took me so far, as I know God's well is never empty.

By the time I was in my early twenties, I had graduated from post-secondary school and started my career in social work. I was living on my own with my boyfriend at the time, making my own money, and it felt great. I had still managed to maintain a long-distance relationship with my mother as she was still living in Florida. My mother at the time was estranged from her husband: my abuser as he was still in jail. At that moment in my life, I felt safe in maintaining our relationship. I chose to try to not bring up my childhood abuse as it only brought up negative feelings and a lot of denial on my mother's end.

It was draining energy that I just didn't want in my life. I really wanted to be like every other young woman I knew and have a mom a real connection, no matter how dysfunctional the relationship seemed. Most of my friends at the time had pretty close relationships with their moms as most still lived with them. Their moms were there for them—the good and the bad—and they had good relationships. From my childhood years up to adulthood, I always felt like a motherless child—that feeling never really left me. However, my grandmother was always there for me and she filled that void. To this day, my grandmother and I still have a very close relationship. I thank God for my grandmother every day.

As dysfunctional as it was to maintain a relationship with someone that abandoned my sister and I as young children, I held on too my mother anyway and grasped on to any form of a relationship. During the time of trying to build a relationship with my mother, a setback happened. Just when things were starting to become somewhat progressive, my mother had made an odd request.

My mother had asked me to write a letter to a judge about my stepfather for he was facing more jail time on a recent charge regarding immigration issues, to my understanding. During the trial for that charge, the previous charges and his past of being in jail for sexual abuse came up. The letter would be a character witness letter describing my stepfather's character, and how despite the sexual abuse, he was a good man. The purpose of this was to let him out of his sentence early or appoint him less time. I was dumbfounded to say the least. How could my mother think that it would be OK for me of all people to write a letter like this? I was hurt and confused. As she continued to talk on the phone about it, I was numb.

I stopped listening at that point and I felt like the world was spinning. All I can remember was that she was trying to convince me that he was a good person and remind me of when he helped me learn my times tables—like that was to make up for the horrific trauma I endured by the hands of this man. All this time I thought we were making progress, but she was clearly still in denial about the abuse. I was highly offended hurt and saddened. I did not write the letter.

My mother, and our relationship, took five hundred steps back. Once again, I felt abandoned by my mother. I asked myself over and over what I did to deserve this. Why did I keep hitting a brick wall with my mother? Later on in my life, I realized my mother was a broken individual; she had no concept of what loving herself meant, so how could she love me? Back then, she did not know how to love me; she was easily controlled and manipulated by my stepfather and that would continue for years to come.

To get over that odd request I decided to detach for some time and have limited interactions with my mother and sweep the incident under the rug. I went on about my life and work; I was still in a relationship with my boyfriend at the time, which would turn emotionally abusive and violent. I was always in control and never thought that I would be a victim of domestic abuse—I thought I was in control and strong. We didn't start out that way, but when I look back, the signs were there. I just chose to ignore them. Ladies, if you find yourself in this predicament, please find help. Don't ignore the signs like I did, confide in someone, and get help. The last straw was when I found out he was cheating on me repeatedly. Our three-year relationship ended; he moved out and I moved on. So with no real relationship with my mother and a recent break up, I felt pretty empty and alone.

As each year passed, I wondered if this was going to be the year that I would lose my mind as the statistics said with the past I had, that was pretty much my outcome. I was about to head straight to the bottle, go into a depression, be riddled with anxiety, go on drugs, and the list goes on. Every birthday that passed, I asked myself if this was it—my breakdown year when it was all going to fall down.

After every setback I had with my mother and my emotional state at the time, I thought, "Yup this is it. Here comes my "break down." Now that I look back at it, this was a form of self-torture. I know now that God was carrying me through my storm. I don't know how I survived or how I even managed to get out of bed in those dark days. Now I know how.

Matthew 11:28-30 says, *"Come to me, all you who are weary and burdened and I will give you rest. Take my yoke upon you and learn from me, for I am gentle and humble in heart, and you will find rest for your souls. For my yoke is easy and my burden is* *light."* This verse is so profound and fitting to the restless stage I was going through at that time. Back then I had no real knowledge of God's love for me, and how he wanted me to unleash all my burdens on him and stop carrying them like a noose around my neck weighing me down. As a survivor of sexual abuse, I felt that way most of the time. I had this label that I couldn't shake. I felt like I was being choked and smothered and that there was no relief or no way out of this pain. I know now that I could release it all to him, for he carried the cross so that I could be free and my chains could be broken.

After that last setback with my mother, I decided to absorb myself into my work and social life—and that's exactly what I did. I was working in the field of social services, and I really enjoyed my job so that kept me quite busy and I loved it! With my job and my social life, my ex was a thing of the past. I never looked back. I figured our relationship was toxic and it so desperately needed to end. Things were going well; I was living as a single woman and making my way through life. I managed once again to salvage some sort of relationship with my mother after the last hiccup. As you can tell, I desperately wanted a mother, so I kept letting her back in even though it was toxic for my soul. I confided in my mother about my ex and the whole process of moving on. She was there for me at that time as a listening ear.

Things were going alright in our mother-daughter relationship; we were making some progress. I began to slowly trust my mother again, so I was opening up. My mother was still living in Florida at the time and she confided in me that she was making plans to move back to Canada. I was looking forward to my mother moving back to Toronto as we would be able to restore some sort of relationship. But, my mother had other intentions. During one of our long distance conversations, she decided to disclose she will be moving back to Canada but nowhere near Toronto. Vancouver, British Columbia was her choice.

I was puzzled. I didn't understand why she would choose to go so far. No one lives in Vancouver—none of our relatives or friends. All of our extended family lives in Toronto, so why so far? Her deciding to move so far away was odd, so I asked her why and I finally got my answer. My mother decided it was time to make her marriage work. Her husband was locked up in prison and soon to be released. Once released, he could no longer stay in the U.S. for fear he would be deported back to Jamaica since he wasn't a U.S citizen.

So, she had been making arrangements to move back to Canada where he was a Canadian citizen—just nowhere near our family. I was once again fuming and felt like such a fool for believing things would be different this time and that we would finally be able to heal. The healing and restoration of our relationship would not take place for years to come. Our conversation that day was filled with frustration and feelings of betrayal on my end. I tried to tell her all kinds of angles: moving back to Toronto would be better for our family, her husband was using her, he is a convicted pedophile, how could you be waiting for him after what he has done to me and our family, and the list went on with the negatives but she was firm on her choice and decided to go on with her decision.

I had two younger sisters and one step sister that would be living with my mom, which are his daughters, and I pleaded with her to not bring that monster around them. I told her to think of me and what I went through. I asked her why was she willing to bring a pedophile around three young girls, even if it's their father? I told her she would be to blame if anything happens to them. She was fully aware of the consequences, but it did not seem to alter her choice.

There was one comment from that conversation, I do remember she made before we hung up that day. She stated, "It's better to know the devil you are dealing with then to not know at all." I had no words at that point. I knew that my mother was lost and in major denial—reasoning with logic wasn't a part of her psyche at the time. I feared for my sisters, knowing that my mother was putting those girls in direct danger bothered me to my core. I just prayed to God that he would protect them and watch over them. I did a lot of soul searching during that time, I knew that this toxic roller coaster I was going through had to end. The relationship with my mother was weighing on my soul and I felt helpless.

The masks that I have been wearing to keep up with this relationship with my mother was slowly starting to slip off. I was tired of pretending everything was ok and being treated this way by my mother was ok. I no longer wanted to accept this fate. At some point or another, you may have worn your own mask—you know the invisible mask we put on just like our favorite lipstick or blush. A lot of us don't even know it's there but it is. It could be a necessity to get through the day. It assures us that we are OK even though we are breaking on the inside wondering when the aching will stop. But it doesn't, so we must keep up the image of perfection to the outside world because being vulnerable is not cute.

With that being said, those images often conflict with our inner being. I know it did for me, already being a young woman who faced a difficult childhood, I felt the need to keep up the strong exterior I had made up for myself. No one was going to even catch a whiff of what I went through and they didn't. However, you can only keep up with this false exterior for so long, until it starts to chip away at you and you grow more and more tired of pretending.

Was it the immaturity in me to try to strive for these ideals? Maybe but that's what I wanted to be: I wanted to look perfect to the outside world. During this time, my relationship with my mother became very strained. The phone calls became brief and very limited as I was trying to distance myself from her toxic grip. I came to the realization that I need to get back on the saddle and seek professional help. I started to go back to counseling on a weekly basis, and I felt connected to this particular counselor; we were making progress and breaking ground.

Through my sessions, the issue of control came up again. Control was my coping mechanism and my crutch to control everything and everyone associated with me. I had this down to a science. My daily planner kept this control habit in check, hour by hour, day by day. I felt I was the one in charge of my life. I was the one calling all the shots, and I was proud of what I had accomplished so far.

My current counselor was very in-tune with my coping mechanism and the daily masks I wore to fool others and myself. You get to a point where you can't even decipher who you really are. The mask and your true self begin to merge—at least it did in my case. Getting to the bottom of who I truly was, would be a major task, but I was ready at this point in my journey. During one of our sessions, my counselor suggested it may be time to explore the idea writing a letter to my mother, releasing the pain in words. At first, I did not feel ready at that point to start the task of writing down all my pain out on paper.

The thought made me ill. However, I said that I would consider it when I was ready. To me, writing all my pain out made it official—speaking them is one thing but writing it out was permanent. When you speak, sometimes it can be forgotten by the other on the receiving end or even twisted around to one's own interpretation.

Words are forever. Once written you cannot take them back—it's permanent. I claimed to have wanted closure, to finally end this dysfunctional relationship, but did I really? Did I really want to let go of my past hurt with my mother? Did I really want to release the crutch, the crutch of being a victim of my circumstances instead of a survivor standing on my own two feet? To me, this would mean no more crutch. No more blame game. No more pointing fingers. No more feeling sorry for myself. No more self-pity. No more control. That is what writing that letter symbolized for me: complete release. It was quite scary, I knew I had to write this letter, so one evening, after ruminating with the idea for weeks, I picked up the pad and pen and wrote and wrote and wrote until my fingers were numb.

I wrote it all leaving nothing out. I put it away for the night and would send it the next day. Some of you may be thinking, *"Wow, you didn't even mull it over for a few days?"* Nope. I was ready. There comes a time in your life when you say enough is enough and its time to make a serious game changing move and this was mine. This letter for me would either make my relationship with my mother or break it.

All my pain was immersed into a three-page letter, and I wanted my voice to be heard and I wanted release. Scared as anything, this was it—no more hiding. I mailed the letter to my mother. I went to work the next day and confided in one of my good girl friends Marisa, who has been with me through this whole roller coaster from beginning to end. She was always there to listen, and I was so appreciative of her support. I found it so important to find people I could be myself around- no mask, no pretending, just be. And I was with her. She saw the raw Sherika— the good, bad, and the ugly—and she will always be a dear friend to me for helping me get through this painful journey.

My mother called me later on that day just to see how my day was going, and I was very brief with her as I was learning to create healthy boundaries. After that brief conversation, that was the last time I would speak to my mother for several years. I decided that once I sent the letter, it would be the last of any form of communication.

I was done. I didn't want to be a victim and to be emotionally drained by trying to stitch together some form of a relationship with my mother. The dysfunction had to end; I had to end it for my own sanity. Once I put that letter into the mailbox, it was like a weight had been literally lifted off of my shoulders. I made peace with it.

And I was going to accept whatever the outcome was. Deep down I hoped that my mother would come to her senses and want to throw away her old life of dysfunction with my stepfather and see that I was worth it. I wanted to be worthy of my mother's love. I wanted her to finally choose me. After all these years of playing second fiddle and feeling less than, I wanted her to choose me. Unfortunately, that day never came until many years later.

It would take a few days for my mother to receive the letter, so I waited and waited. Finally, I got a response but not the one I was hoping for. I really thought that this would be it, that I would finally have my happy ending and my mom would be willing to start a real relationship with me but on my terms, the one that I had laid out in the letter. After all, if I just made her see in writing plain as day, she would see that I am worth it. To my dismay, I could not control this. I had no control over my mother. Again my controlling issues were creeping to the surface.

The girl who thought she could be in control of every aspect of her life had absolutely none over this. I was at a loss. I took a gamble, and I had to face the outcome. So, if I had no control over this situation then God surely did. I became angrier for it. I cried out to God, *"Why are you doing this to me? Why am I a motherless child? Why doesn't she love me?"* I felt very alone.

My mother had decided to leave several messages on my phone. The messages consisted of major denial on her part and by no means was she going to dismantle her life to maintain a relationship with me. So, I did what I knew I had to do: cut off communication. To save my sanity and myself from any more emotional trauma, the cord had to be cut. A week later I had my counseling session where we discussed the outcome of this. I felt I lost my mother.

But, did I really have her? I had a false sense of a mother. I crafted together one in my mind and put together pieces of my mother to suit my expectations. During this time in my life, I still had a close relationship with my maternal grandmother. She stepped in and filled that void for me. She was there for me in all aspects, and I thank God for that connection—it will always be dear to my heart. My grandmother was not perfect, but I knew she loved me. She showed me love and I never felt abandoned. That's all I ever wanted, to not feel like a motherless child and she did the best she could as a grandmother to a granddaughter.

I told my grandmother everything that had transpired, for she knew that I was writing the letter to my mother. Somehow my mother decided to blame my grandmother for the letter as if she orchestrated the whole ordeal. This was far from the truth. This was my decision and my decision alone.

I really could not see God's plan at the time. Controlling Sherika had to sit back and let God take over. As painful as it was, I had to take a seat. Sometimes we can only go so far with our own strength, and I was running on fumes. I had no energy to fight this battle on my own. I was tapped out. So as bull headed as I was, I surrendered willingly for once in my life to let go and let God take over.

One thing I have learned on this life journey is that when you fully submit to God, you will see his best work transpire before your eyes. As people we can be so adamant about achieving or succeeding on our own will, when in retrospect he is the one that will carry you to achievements and places you can only imagine if you submit and let him take over.

So, I let him take over. Now, the thing about fully submitting is to know that whatever the outcome, is it's his will. Sometimes we don't see his plan come to pass immediately; it may take days, months, or even years. In my case it took years. Patience is a virtue. In seeing God's plan for me come together, I had to be very patient. God knows that's not one of my strengths (I pray for gallons of patience every day). Still, I stayed faithful and waited for his plan for me to one day be revealed. I was learning to let go and no longer have a victim mentality. I was slowly moving towards becoming the victor, the survivor. I took a huge leap of faith writing that letter to my mother and finally releasing control. The mind shift from victim to survivor had begun.

Chapter 5

IN GOD'S TIME, ALL WILL BE REVEALED

"She holds
on to hope
for he is
forever faithful."

~ 1 Corinthians 1:9

God's timing is always perfect; I mean literally every time. When we wait on him to deliver what needs to be done in whatever circumstances in our lives, it always seems to unfold the way it's supposed to. Being estranged from my mother was hard. There is no easy way to put it. Cutting off all communication from my mother, although our relationship was toxic for me, was one of the hardest things I could have ever done. I knew I had to do it, but when you are in it, it's a whole other battle. So despite me wanting to rekindle a relationship with my mother, I didn't. I remained firm in my decision and hoped one day things would be different.

During those years that my mother was absent from my life, I was actually doing pretty well. I began dating an amazing man, who showed me so much unconditional love that three years later I married him and became his wife. Christopher Powell was my best friend, and I was so blessed to be marrying such an amazing person. His kind and gentle nature was so invigorating; he was exactly the kind of soul mate I needed. I knew I wanted to get married one day and have an everlasting love, but with what I was exposed to in my life I wasn't sure that I would get my prince charming. But he arrived and I knew that I would want to spend the rest of my life with him. He has seen me at my very best and my very worst, and while we were dating I didn't think he would have wanted to continue our relationship. I thought that once he knew about my past, he would have thought of me as damaged goods. But he saw past all of that, he saw so much more than that and I am so thankful for it. He picked me up when I was down and was there for me with all the tribulations with my mother. He held me and wiped all my tears. I knew our bond was sacred and a forever kind of love. While we were going through our wedding details, I decided that it was best that my mother did not attend my wedding as I was estranged from her.

Christopher understood my position and understood why she wouldn't be there. The wedding day went off without a hitch! Everyone probably says this about their wedding, but it was the best day of our lives! All of our family and friends celebrated the night away—it was pure bliss and we couldn't be happier. Right after the wedding, we were off to beautiful Mexico for our honeymoon. It was just paradise. I loved this man with every being in me—we were a God union, soul mates, which are so rare to find. But God was looking after me. He knew the kind of husband I would need: someone who was understanding, patient, kind, gentle, and who just adored me! Despite my flaws, and I have a lot of them, and despite my past and what I went through, he just simply loved me and that's all I ever wanted. Once we came back from the honeymoon, it was back to real life and life as newlyweds. Things were good; we were transitioning into husband and wife quite nicely.

Soon after, I found out I was expecting our first child together. We were very excited! I was also very nervous about becoming a mother. Flashbacks started to haunt me from my childhood, and I became fearful and scared and wondered if history would repeat itself. Would I be a replica of my mother? I had no example of what a mother should be. Would I be neglectful? Would I physically and verbally abuse my children? I prayed that I would not pick up those negative traits and rise above them. It was February 22nd, 2010 when I finally gave birth to my baby boy Jacob (and two years later I would give birth to my second son, Christopher; both these boys are my heart). I was in love.

The abundant love I felt for this child was just amazing. I stared down at his perfect little hands and toes and beautiful face and saw pure joy. I thought to myself, *"Wow, I could and would never let anything come into harm's way of this precious gift."* God chose me to be his mother and he makes no mistakes so therefore I was equipped for the job. I may stumble, I may fall down on the journey of motherhood, but I knew God would carry me through. During Jacob's first year of life, I was trying this motherhood thing on for size, getting to know my little one and myself as a mother. It came with its challenges but I loved it. I did wish back then I had a mother there to guide me, to tell me what it would be like, what to look out for with my new born and to just talk.

As dysfunctional as my mother was at the time, I still longed for that connection. My maternity leave had ended, and it was time for me to go back to work, which was bittersweet. We had planned a trip to Florida later on that year, and I was really looking forward to the much needed break. When we arrived and got settled something transpired that I knew only God could have orchestrated. We had been on the trip for a few days when the hotel phone rang, and it was for me. My mother was on the other end of the line. Yes, my mom—the one who I hadn't spoken to for several years was on the other end of the phone. I had no relationship with her whatsoever; we were practically strangers. My mother began begging and pleading that I do not hang up the phone. Hanging up the phone was actually my first instinct as I was on vacation, and I did not want any negative energy on my trip. I then began to wonder what could it be? Was my grandmother ill? Did something happen to one of my siblings? I thought those would be the only reasons why she would be calling me all the way from Florida.

She then began to speak and sob in a way that was painful to hear. She was pleading for my forgiveness and expressed how sorry she was that she had abandoned me all these years: she had seen the light. Her marriage with my stepfather was crumbling, and she was filing for a divorce. She expressed that she realized how wrong she was to have neglected me and chosen her husband over me—her husband who sexually abused her daughter. She was sorry and wanted my forgiveness. I sat there silently on the phone. I did not say a word during the whole conversation.

I just listened. After she was done, I told her that I couldn't comment at this time but I would call her once I returned home. She understood and hung up. I thought to myself, *"Hmm now this is a God moment. It was time, and a shift was about to happen in my life."* I shared what had just transpired over the phone with my husband, and he was shocked—actually we both were! But man, God surely does work on his time because it is always the right time. God knew that it would take several years of estrangement from my mother for me to be ready to receive what was coming to me on that day. During those years of no communication with my mother, I was on a mission to know God on a more personal level.

I wanted and craved that connection. Looking back, I truly believe it was all preparation for the day my mother came back into my life and to see if I would be truly ready to receive it and forgive. Had I not been on the journey of getting to know Christ, I truly believe that I would not have been ready to receive my mother and her request of forgiveness. I had returned home from our trip, and I was ready to have that hard conversation with my mother. I knew that one conversation would not change everything, but it had to begin somewhere.

Over the course of several months, my mother and I would have multiple lengthy conversations about the past, about what I had encountered in relation to the sexual abuse, and so on. I laid it all out and talked about how much pain was caused by her hands and my stepfather's. She listened to me and just let me vent. She finally understood after all these years where I was coming from. My mother decided to end her 15-year marriage because she had put up with being manipulated and emotionally abused for years. She revealed that things with her were not good for a very long time, and she finally decided to leave after she found out he was having an affair along with the emotional abuse.

She decided to move out, find her own place with my younger sisters, and work on herself. Like I stated before, I couldn't believe it! I thought I would never speak to my mother again, and I would just live my life not having a mother—I had accepted that in my heart. I wanted to protect myself, so I just continued on with life like she didn't exist. She said she began attending counselling, which helped her to see more clearly the choices she was making in her life. I was still very cautious of my mother; I did not fully trust her.

I mean, who could blame me, she was like a stranger. I decided to pray on it a lot and let her in to my life, piece by piece. I was nervous—was this real? Or was this another scenario where this was going to blow up in my face again? I was skeptical. As time went on, the tough exterior on my heart began to chip away, and I realized my mother was going from victim to survivor. My mother, due to her own circumstances that transpired in her past life, did not know how to love me the way I wanted a mother to love me when I was a child. This took time for me to process and was hard for me to swallow at times because my mom was also a victim of her circumstances.

Does it excuse her behavior? Not at all, but I got a better understanding of where she was coming from. Although she declared that she loved me and always did, and even though we didn't speak for many years, it was her definition of love, not mine. I found it hard to believe that you could love someone and abuse and neglect them the way that I was, but I can't control the way another person defines love. I listened to my mother's stance on things and how she learned to live with herself and the choices she made at the time.

She told me she did not have an easy life with her soon-to-be ex, and she was the victim of emotional abuse and manipulation. I began to see my mother in a different light; I no longer saw her as the woman who was a part of my abuse but also a victim to her circumstance. My mother declared that she was walking in a fog for so many years and finally the blinders were off. She was ready to face the consequences of her mistakes. It took everything in me to believe her; it was very hard. I was a wounded soul that feared being hurt again and let down by my mother. I knew, though, that in order for me to heal, I needed to truly be open to having a relationship and learn to forgive her over time. Believe me, this was no small task. It took me a very long time to come to a place where I no longer felt betrayed and angry.

I truly believe that I could not have gone through that difficult phase in my life without God comforting my spirit and showing me the way. Without God's grace, I would not have forgiven my mother; I am sure of that. I am still in awe of what God can do if you believe and let him in. If you would have told me that I would have a relationship with my mother again, and would be able to forgive her and my stepfather for what they have done, I would have never believed you. But because his grace is sufficient and more than enough, that too is possible! God's plans for our lives are beyond what we can see. In his timing God reveals all things, and it's right on time!

Chapter 6

The Dreaded "F" Word: Forgiveness

"Forgive others
not because they
deserve forgiveness
but because you
deserve peace"

~ Jonathan Lockwood Huie

Ephesians 4:32

"Be kind to one another, tender-hearted, forgiving one another, as God in Christ forgave you."

When I first read this verse, I was not so quick to oblige. I mean, God, really? Everyone, do you really mean everyone?! He couldn't possibly. Maybe there is fine print in the bible somewhere just for me saying, *"Forgive except mothers who are neglectful and stepfathers who are sexually abusive."* Nope, it didn't say that anywhere—no special foot note for me, no fine print. So, I had to marinate on that one for a long time; it did not come easy. But for me to free myself from mental bondage, it had to be done. Forgiving those that have hurt you, abused you, and neglected you is a personal decision that can only be made between you and God.

For so many years I had been struggling with the notion of forgiveness. I heard it so many times, said in so many ways, on when and how to forgive. I just didn't get it. Why should I forgive my then step father who raped and sexually assaulted me? Why should I forgive my neglectful mother? Why? I held on to that for years. I would not give them the satisfaction of "forgiving" them! They were the cause of all my pain.

I decided I would not let them win. I was going to carry this hurt and pain to my grave—I vowed I would. I really thought people were insane when I would watch talk shows or listen to radio shows and the guests or the speakers would be talking about forgiving the perpetrators that victimized them. They expressed by doing this act of forgiveness, they felt like they had been set free, and they were no longer prisoners of the person who victimized them—by forgiving them, they had taken away their power. I had a hard time grasping that concept. During the stage of my life as the "victim," I was nowhere near the space of forgiving anyone. The one thing I hated hearing was you must forgive no matter what has been done wrong to you. This made me feel like the horror I had encountered in my young childhood was something that I needed to just accept and move on from. I saw forgiveness as a sign of weakness. I felt that those who chose to forgive, in any circumstances, were weak. This attitude spilled over to my personal life with friends and family; I had no room for error.

With that being said, a few relationships back then could have probably been salvaged if I had made room in my heart for forgiveness. Why was I looking for perfection in others when I didn't even have it myself? I didn't give people an option to disappoint me more than once. I had been there way too many times in my past that I wasn't going to let it into my future. I trusted people very little as they often disappointed me.

Psalm 118:8 says, *"It is better to trust in the LORD than to put confidence in man."* I later realized that people are going to let you down they are going to disappoint you and hurt you. But God will never forsake you, I learned that lesson way later on in life. At the time, I was putting a lot of weight on relationships especially toxic ones. I didn't understand the word forgiveness—it was like speaking another language. I didn't understand how to forgive or what it meant. Later on in life, as I became more interested in my faith, the topic of forgiveness came up quite often.

In time, and as I increased my walk with Christ, I have been able to forgive my abuser and my mother. I, in turn, have felt a huge weight being lifted off my shoulders. Now forgiving doesn't mean you forget by any means, but the bitterness and the hate that you use to carry around is released. Bitterness in your heart will consume you in more ways than one—believe me, I know from experience. Now, that being said, this does not mean people who have hurt you, will become your best friend and you will be singing kumbaya together.

That is not what forgiveness means. You forgive because at some point you realize the past is just that, the past, and you can't change it. Holding on to the past and what was will not bring you any closer to the future. The future that God has in store for you is bright, so bright! So do not let anyone steal your joy and all the plans God has in store for you. Forgiveness is such a personal decision, that in my opinion, it can only be done with God by your side giving you the strength to do so. With him all things are possible, and I am a living witness to that. My life revealed on these pages is a witness to the fact that forgiveness can be done.

Most of you may wonder what my relationship is presently like with my mother. I can tell you that it has manifested into something that only God's hand can be in. I am so grateful for our relationship; now my mother and I talk frequently and more than ever I see a woman who is far from perfect, but a work in progress. Do I wish all the hurdles with my mother and I never transpired? Certainly! But when I look back, I see how those hurdles where equipping me with the tools and the knowledge to pursue this purpose and this platform. Who would have thought after years of estrangement, my mother and I would be back to rekindling a relationship!

We are in a great place; she is the mother I never had, and I feel blessed. God's time is always the right time, and no task is too big for him. Forgiveness is possible—if we attempt to forgive on our own strength, many times over, we will fail. But through his grace and mercy, we can find compassion in our hearts to forgive those who hurt us along the way.

Chapter 7

BECOMING UNCHAINED

"We are all broken that's how the light gets in."

~ Ernest Hemingway

What does becoming unchained mean to you? Well, for me, it meant finally becoming free from my past pain, heartache, and disappointment. It meant removing the tightly wound noose around my neck that was just about to suck the life out of me. I didn't think I would ever get there; I thought my soul would be restless forever. At that time, my life was bleak. I filled those days with parties, drinking, and careless behavior just to numb the pain of my reality. I thought I would find it in people and friendships: my inner peace and a sense of belonging. I never found it until years later the chains were finally broken. My unchaining moment didn't happen overnight—it was a gradual chipping away at the tough exterior I showed the world. Little did everyone know, I was still the scared and ashamed little girl.

I finally realized that I am not in control of my life and the purpose God has for it. The series of unchaining moments happened after the birth of my second son, Christopher.

This new little bundle of joy just melted my heart. I was in love all over again. Unfortunately, shortly after giving birth to little Christopher, I had a few complications that landed me in the hospital a week after giving birth. I was scared and the whole ordeal shuck me to me core. My heart wasn't beating as it was supposed to, and I had to be monitored. At first, they thought it could be a blood clot and I panicked; I knew what that meant, and I was very scared. However, God is good and all my tests for blood clots came back negative. But, my heart was still beating irregularly.

I was finally released from the hospital and was able to hold my baby. With some follow-up with cardiologists, I was getting back to my normal self and my heart began to beat as it normally should. That ordeal, knowing that it could have gone another way, made me grateful for my life, my breath, and being. It was then when I completely and whole heartedly took Jesus as my Lord and savior and became baptized that year. I felt a sense of calm come over my spirit like no other. All the tears I cried, sleepless nights, and the shame of my past, all of it was wiped away. He took it all and set me free from my chains. They were finally broken. I finally became unchained. Now I still had, and have, moments of fear, worry, and anxiety, but the difference is now I know where to put my faith and trust; I leave it at the cross.

I tried throughout all my years as a young girl, teenager, and young adult to go through this world on my own strength. I did not succeed. I ended up making wrong choices, getting involved with the wrong relationships, and becoming toxic. I was in mental turmoil. Looking back on my life, I can say that God can make anything possible! I am a living witness to that. I wonder to myself how on earth I survived this. All the odds were against me; I shouldn't have survived this by human standards! But his grace is sufficient.

Boy, is it ever! He brought me through this, and by the grace of Jesus I am here sharing my testimony with you. I know you must hear this phrase often: *"All things are possible with God,"* but I am here to say they really are! Without him, I am, and would be, nothing. Through him, I have the courage to write my experience in this book and have decided to no longer be silent and share it with the world. My hope through this journey is not only that I am healed by this experience but also that someone else is healed and ready to make some big moves in their lives. I hope through sharing my experiences that someone is ready to let God really and truly move into their lives and finally become unchained!

Years ago I did not behave or act like someone who loved herself. I didn't feel like I was worthy of loving myself, when I felt at the time God did not love me, for I was damaged goods. I was used and abused. Self-love was a strange concept. I know now that in order to be a healthy person, self-love must exist. And when you truly grasp that concept and realize you are loved so deeply by your creator, it is an exhilarating feeling. When love of one's self is absent, negative thoughts and behaviors often creep into our minds and we actually believe them. Then we act on them and our negative view of ourselves becomes our reality.

Whether it be not loving yourself enough to leave toxic relationships or situations, self-love is a key component to becoming awakened and seeing your life differently the way God sees it: beautiful. For me, self-love took time to build. Through the trauma I experienced as a child, my tank was darn near empty. I had to start from the ground up and do a lot of soul searching to learn to love what I saw staring back at me in the mirror—all of it! From my eyes to my nose to my thick lips to the shape of my body I had to learn to see beauty they way God saw it when he created me. For many years, I did not like the person in the mirror.

I thought she wasn't worthy of self-love or true love because of her broken past. But because God is such an amazing God, full of grace, he gently nudged me to the side of self-acceptance and love. He gently whispered, "You are loved," and over the years my mind shifted gears, and I realized I am a child of God. I realized that my past does not dictate my future. I realized my lord and savior loves me too much to leave me in this state of self-pity. I was ready to get up, brush myself off, and see myself made in his image imperfectly perfect.

As women, we can be highly critical of ourselves and this world doesn't make it easy for us. We are bombarded on a daily basis with images of what beauty looks like in the standards of the world. Getting to that place of real self-love is a personal and rewarding journey. Not only will you learn to like the reflection that is staring back at you in the mirror but you will finally feel this inner peace that only God can create. The peace in knowing you are more than enough, and all the trials and tribulations you have endured up to this point in your life were never wasted. It is all a part of the journey of finding the beauty that lies within all women. You can't go through this life without having some battle wounds, but rest assured in knowing that God saw you through it all. You are his creation, flaws and all, and he sees you as simply beautiful.

As women we need to be careful to not fall into the comparison trap: I'm not as pretty as another woman, or I am not as talented as another woman. There is no point in women comparing ourselves to one another. God does not compare his designs with one another. He sees us as unique, beautiful beings. He holds each one of us so high and loves exactly what he made. Let's hold our heads up high and be glad in what God created us to be: beautiful, strong, victorious, courageous women — unchained!

Chapter 8

FINDING PURPOSE IN THE PAIN

"You were put on this earth to achieve your greatest self, to live out your purpose, and to do it courageously."

~ Steven Maraboli

The Oxford dictionary defines purpose as, *"The reason for which something exists or is done, made, used, etc. an intended or desired result; end; aim; goal."* I firmly believe this is my purpose. Using this platform to reach others with my testimony and giving a voice to the voiceless is my purpose. I am using my past pain to restore my purpose on this earth. No longer will I keep silent about the real tragedy of childhood sexual abuse. It is real. I am a part of the statistic.

But I do not, and will not, keep silent any longer. I believe my purpose is solely to show other women that the more we speak out about this epidemic, the more strength we have to stop this crime against girls and women. I never in my wildest dreams would have thought that my journey and my past pain would lead me to share my story candidly with you. But I have made a decision that I will chose to be a victorious warrior for this cause. There were many times in my life

---

In Canada, one in three girls by the age of 18 have been sexually assaulted.
http://littlewarriors.ca/about/regional/statistics-research/)

when I thought, what is the point of my life? Why did God spare me? This life he has given me is a gigantic waste and mess!

Those thoughts kept me silent, negative, bound, and full of hate. But when the blinders come off and the light is revealed, and all the lies the devil has told you all your life are smashed in a million pieces, what an exhilarating feeling! He told me I could never be loved (big lie, I'm married to the love of my life), he told me I would never be successful (big lie, I define my success and I lead a very successful life), he told me my mother and I would never have a relationship again (big lie, my mother and I now have a great relationship and I love her), and he told me my past pain would ruin me (big lie, not only has it not ruined me, I'm using it to help others).

All of these lies have kept me in mental bondage for so many years, and you may have had these lies swirl around in your head as well. I'm a living witness that your life your journey is neither a waste of time nor is it useless in God's eyes. Every adversity you have faced is all useful. When the storms come and you feel like the wheels are spinning out of control; you feel like you can't go on, and this life is torturing you. That's when it's time to get down on your knees and talk to him; I mean really talk to him—pour out your deepest inner thoughts to God. He is listening ready and waiting to show you your next path.

Philippians 3:12-14 says, *"I'm not saying that I have this all together, that I have it made. But I am well on my way, reaching out for Christ, who has so wondrously reached out for me. Friends, don't get me wrong: By no means do I count myself an expert in all of this, but I've got my eye on the goal, where God is beckoning us onward-to Jesus. I'm off and running and I'm not turning back."* I can really resonate with this verse; it captures exactly where I am and where I am going. Christ reached out to me and plucked me out of the darkness, shook me off, and told me I have a job to do. Not only did he release me from my brokenness, but, in turn, my brokenness will now be used to release people from their chains. I am made whole in Christ.

I am no longer bound I am ready to be unleashed and set free. Now, God did not say the road to the journey of following his path for your life would be an easy task. Believe me, the task of writing this book has been years in the making with a lot of hurdles and bumps along the way. But every time there was a setback, I stayed firm in his promises to me, that despite all of my battles I will come out victorious, courageous, and stronger than I ever was! I truly believe that because there is no way God was not present through my journey, carrying and lifting me to higher ground. His plans for my life were great even when I didn't know it. When you stay obedient to his calling and really pay attention to where he is directing you, there are things he has in store for you that you cannot imagine: he is ready to take you higher! But, are you ready to go with him?

The purpose driven life is no small journey. When you are ready to get serious about where God is taking you, hold on to your seat—it's going to be a bumpy ride! Let God show you that your life is not wasted—not the past, present, or future. We all have a purpose; it is divine and unique a perfect fit for every human being on the planet. No purpose is exactly alike, and that's what makes it worth going after. Just like in my life, he has a lot of beautiful things in store for yours: you are worthy, you are courageous, and, above all, you are loved by the creator.

Jerimiah 29:11 says, *"For I know the plans I have for you, declares the Lord, plans to prosper and not to harm you, to give* *you hope and a future."* Isn't this a beautiful promise by God? He knows the plans he has in store for us, and there lies hope and a new future. I didn't know what my future held back then. I didn't know what more tragedies and hopeless nights I would encounter as the road I was on was the least desirable one, in my eyes. I felt God really had forgotten about me and, at the time, I felt very alone.

Around my friends and family, I seemed well and quite happy, but they were not around when I was alone with my dark thoughts just me, myself, and I. When you have no concept of God's love, the world can be a lonely place. When I look back on what God has brought me through, wow, God really is a modern day miracle worker. Those of you who are reading this book and may have gone through something like my story or similar, I am here to tell you that a new beginning is on the horizon for you. I hope that in sharing my life journey, you can see that it is possible for a new beginning. You are exactly where you are supposed to be right now in your life, and the Lord is guiding and walking with you every step of the way. Whether you are at a difficult bump or a smooth journey, he is there prepping you for your new beginning.

Now that I have gone through a little bit of life, I can tell you that getting to that new beginning and awakening can only happen with some disappointments, bumps, and hurdles along the way. You aren't living life if you haven't gotten a few bruises along the way! But, often times, those disappointments and hurt are disguised as wise life lessons that you will need to get you on track to your awakening and enlightenment. While I was going through the most difficult time in my life, I never thought that a new beginning would be in store for me. But the more I learned about Christ's love for me and how much he sacrificed for me, I knew I could face another day!

Our God is bigger than any situation we could ever go through; with his grace, we can endure! Let's turn our darkest hours into something positive; let's help encourage and inspire one another as women. Are we perfect? No, but God never asks us to be perfect—that is his job. Our job is to love, share, and uplift our fellow woman. God gives his fiercest battles to his strongest warriors, and if you believe that phrase, you know you too can turn everything that was meant to destroy you into good and for his glory. So, take the time and think back on your own personal journey.

Think back on all the hurdles, battles, and storms that have happened over the course of your life. At the time you were going through that rough season, I'm sure you thought that it would never end and there was no way out. Yet, here you are, you pushed past the struggles, and, whether you think so or not, you are moving forward. God's hand was there all along moving you forward to get you to your new beginning.

I can tell you from experience that when you truly believe that God is in this life journey with you, and he will never ever forsake you even in your darkest hour, the world starts to look differently. People start to look differently and situations, trials that you still may face begin to look differently. God has our back! He can and will turn your tragedy into triumph! You can overcome any obstacle that is thrown your way because he knows what's in store for your life: a blessed journey only if you believe and let him in. Through my journey I have realized nothing was in vain, and I have found purpose in the pain.

Chapter 9

IF YOUR DREAMS DON'T SCARE YOU,
THEY AREN'T BIG ENOUGH.

"Feel the Fear and do it anyway."

~ Susan Jeffers

My dreams scared me—I mean literally paralyzed me. The concept of writing my story, becoming an author, and sharing my personal journey of my life was earth shattering to me. I remember when I first got a glimpse of God's vision for my life, my calling, and what I was put on this earth to do. It was a rainy day in May that changed my life forever. I had just finished my maternity leave, and I was headed back to work. I was driving into work when the vision for my life flashed before my eyes. Like it was a movie: I saw the name of the book, the colors I was going to use on the cover, and that I was going to write my story in a book. All the hairs on my arms stood up as I knew this revelation was for me. When I got the revelation, I told God numerous times that I was not up to the task or equipped.

It's funny how we immediately disqualify ourselves when we get called to do something out of our comfort zone. The wall immediately goes up and we say, *"No way not me!"* I was disqualifying myself gladly because really, didn't God see how busy of a woman I was? I laid out every reason under the sun why he shouldn't choose me for this task, and the list goes a little something like this!

1. I have no time.

2. I am a very busy woman with a full agenda to prove it!

3. I have two sons under the age of four.

4. I am a working mom (God, why couldn't you have given me this assignment when I was young and childless!!)

5. I don't know how to write a book.

6. I don't think my message is book worthy.

7. I am not the creative type.

8. And again I asked, "God don't you see how busy I am?"

That was my list, my false script that I kept playing over and over in my head, letting God know (as if this was a surprise to him) that I am not the one and to pick someone else. This went on for months; I didn't budge and I didn't do anything with the vision I was given. I was still trying to disqualify myself. However, over those months, it seemed that there were signs everywhere that he wanted to use my past life and share my story with the world. God's plan was going to come into being.

Now I realize God wanted to give hope, faith, and inspiration to women who felt like they had no voice; through my story, he wanted me to be that voice. At last, I surrendered and decided to embrace my assignment and get to work. How does one start writing? Well, just like that— by putting pen to paper. And, that I did. I wrote every free chance I got: I wrote on my memo pad and on my phone, that's actually where most of this book was written, literally paragraphs at a time on my phone. I didn't own a laptop at the time so my only personal keyboard was on my phone.

It became pretty convenient though as soon as I had a thought to write I just quickly jotted it down. Needless to say I finally got that laptop! Being a wife, mom of two boys, working full time and just trying to maintain a household all the while writing a book had its challenges to say the least. Many times I found myself sitting on the floor of my walk in closet with my laptop on my lap writing away. I then realized, *"hmm I'm getting a lot of writing done here in this closet and my kids don't seem bother to look for me in the closet. I mean why would mommy be in the closet?"* So, I made that my hiding place to write a few paragraphs, and when I was done, I headed back to mommy hood! But, eventually I got found out by my youngest son, Christopher, and he would often sit with me amongst the clothes and shoes with a toy of his own and wait until I finished a paragraph or two. I guess you could say he was my little co-author in this process! By any means necessary, I was going to write this book, and if I'm sitting on the floor in my closet, with my son then so be it! God always makes a way!

Writing this book was an intense journey of recalling the past, revealing old wounds, and exposing them for the greater cause. I realized my journey is not my own, but for the women in the world—to give them hope that there is life after abuse or trauma of any kind and God can heal all wounds.

I think as people we can tend to disqualify ourselves from the earth shattering goals. We often say *"Oh, no not me. Oh, please I couldn't do that. Nope, try her over there. I'm not built for that!"* But, why not you? What qualifies you more than the next person? They have a vision, a goal that God put inside of them just as he has done with you. But, what is the difference in achieving them? Well they decided to activate their faith! They decided to take action and soar to new heights. Walt Disney once said, *"All our dreams can come true if we have the courage to pursue them."*

In order to go after our dreams, we need large doses of courage on a daily basis. So, where does one find this courage? Well, for me it was in the Holy Spirit that lives within me. *"I can do all things through Christ who strengthens me,"* **Phillipians 4:13.**

I love this verse; it's one of my favorite affirmations that I repeat daily. Through his abundant strength and grace, I am strong. Many times I wanted to give up, I wanted to throw in the towel and say that this is too hard, I wanted to give up on the vision, and I wanted to quit. I must admit I did quit a few times, but every time I had a stumble God was right there to catch me.

The Lord renewed my strength to go on because this book, my message, was greater than me. In turn God was going to use my journey to restore, hope, faith, love, and inspiration. If I told you pursuing your dreams was easy, I would be lying. It's going to be a journey; it's going to take you on some highs, lows, winding roads, hills, and some forks in the road. However, it is worth sticking it out and seeing your dreams come to being. Nothing worth having comes easy. But, one truth I know well is that through it all, God never leaves your side. He knows the plans he has in store for you; he is just waiting for you to activate your faith.

"Faith without works is dead," **James 2:26.**

If you want God to take you higher, you must activate your steps. We all have unique, amazing gifts. God makes no cookie cutters! Just raw uniqueness. Aren't you ready to find out what yours is? Aren't you ready to explore your vision and manifest the blue print for your life? If so, we must put in the actions to do so the rest will follow. That being said, I think it is so important to have your team in order when you are on this purpose and passion filled journey. Having key players to help get you to the next level is so important.

If you have ever watched Saturday Night Live over the years, you know there is a character called Debbie Downer. She is the kind of girl who sees everything in life as half empty. It's always a bad day in her world. Watching the Debbie Downer character on television is quite humorous, but not so humorous when you are frequently dealing with these kind of people in your life. We have all experienced people like this from time to time in our lives, whether they are co-workers, bosses, friends, relatives, or acquaintances— they do exist. Another name for this type is "dream killers."

The ones who always think your head is in the clouds, or to tell you your ambitions are a waste of time, you need to realize that these kinds of people can be stifling your dreams. This type of person will not add anything of value to your goal-setting journey. They will sink you to the bottom as fast as the titanic. Like attracts like, I am a firm believer in that. Once you start making positive choices about the kinds of conversations you have and who surrounds you, you will begin to see God's light shine on you like on a beautiful sunny day!

I have been blessed with an amazing supportive husband, and I thank God every day for our blessed union. Along with that, a wonderful family and some great girlfriends! This team that I have created has boosted me up, listened to my 101 ideas, and encouraged my journey every step of the way! I am so thankful for God's unions, unions that God puts into place to strengthen you, renew your spirit, and encourage your walk. When I felt like I couldn't go on and my burden was too heavy, this team encouraged me with guidance and love; they encouraged me to keep the faith.

With that being said, if you haven't done so already, start creating your team. Seek out the goal setters, bold movers, achievers, deep thinkers, and encouragers. Start aligning yourself with these team players, and you will see how you begin to change for the better when you surround yourself with positivity. **Ecclesiastes 4: 9-10** says, *"It's better to have a partner than go alone. Share the work share the wealth. And if one falls down, the other helps but if there is no one to help tough!"*

Building your team is essential to your ultimate growth. I also can't stress enough how important your energy space is and who you allow into it on a daily basis. Negative energy is catchy; just as much as positive ones are! Having positive, uplifting people around you while you are moving towards your destiny is crucial. Your team will either make you or break you it's that simple. We cannot do this life alone. We all need support, guidance, and a helping hand to guide us in our seasons of life. We all need that cheering squad to take us higher or even one single cheerer. It only takes one positive influence to set you straight.

Another way to get in alignment with your vision is to do just that, visualize your next move, your next journey! Seeing it can make it seem a lot more real and tangible. One way I do that is through vision boards. I have started taking my vision board seriously over the last few years and have seen a lot of my goals come to reality. What is a vision board? Well, a vision board is a board you create anytime of the year (I prefer the new year). You use it to visualize through magazine images, inspirational quotes, and pictures of what you want your year to look like— it's a collage of goals and aspirations. So when I started a few years ago, I started with some magazines, a board, some glue, and I started creating.

I loved what I saw looking back at me on the board and because I am a visual learner, this helped me stay on track. Visualizing your ultimate goals is so motivating, but those goals can't complete themselves! Prioritizing and careful planning will assist in getting you where you want to be. I had put one goal on my vision board for 2015, which was to be on TV. Now, my interpretation of that was to be interviewed on TV as a guest with regards to talking about my upcoming book. Well, did God have different plans for me! During late 2015, I was told by my good girlfriend Heather (she is the ultimate goal achiever) that I should think about being on TV as a host of my own show. I laughed it off and said, *"Nah, that's not for me. I'm not the right fit for television"* (again disqualifying myself).

The conversation passed, but I always had it in the back of my mind wondering, *"hmm, is she right? Should I attempt this?"* So, I said what is the worst that could happen? They reject me? Big deal (if you are on this journey of actualizing you dreams; you must be OK with getting a lot of "no's"). So, I sent the proposal request to Rogers TV, a local cable channel where they produce community shows. Mind you, this is highly competitive as they receive hundreds of show proposals. One day, I gave it a shot: I went on their website, filled out the proposal for the idea of my show pressed send and forgot about it.

I went about my daily life not thinking about it, not wondering about it. I was OK with the outcome either way. Until a few months later I got an email, indicating that they were interested in my show proposal. What!! Me?? My Show?? Why are we so surprised when we speak things into the universe and they actually happen? I smiled looked up and said, *"OK, God, that was you, I see you."* I went to the meeting. It went well and they told me that the show still needs to be reviewed by the rest of the producers and the decision will be made in a few weeks. So I waited, and a few weeks later I got an email saying my show has been approved! What!! Me? My Show?? I'm going to be a TV talk show host! I smiled up and said, *"Thank you, Lord. I see your vision."* As I write this, I will be the T.V talk show host of Women on the Rise for Rogers Television in Durham Region.

By society's standards, I'm unqualified. I have never been to broadcasting school and never took a journalism or media class. My qualifications don't match up to the industry standards. But when God qualifies you, no man, and I mean no man, can disqualify you! Doors will open and pathways will be made for you that didn't exist otherwise.

172 | A WOMAN UNCHAINED

Why? Because God is in it and he is showing up for you—God's got this!

Be Fearless:

"If God is with us who can be against us," says **Romans 8:31.** If you believe that verse, then why be fearful? Why not take risks, step out of the boat like Peter did to meet Jesus in the storm, and just believe. God has you. Will you stumble, trip, and fall flat on your face? Perhaps, but those hurdles are equipping you for the blessing that is waiting. Through this journey of sharing my life with you, I had to be fearless and trust God's ultimate plan. I had to stay prayed up, dig deep, and walk through territory that I was very unfamiliar with. I had to get uncomfortable before I got comfortable; there were many growing pains.

Every situation, trial, and tribulation was all a part of the bigger picture. Did I ever dream that the little girl who was abused and felt less than worthy half the time would be where I am today? Never! I never thought that one day I would turn my love of reading author's books and admiring their work into one day being an author myself. I couldn't have ever dreamed that up on my own; God knew my outcome—he knew what I was going to be called and used for good later on in my life. If someone told me that this was going to be my destiny, I would have laughed out loud! However, God knew and he qualified me anyway. God is ready to qualify you! He is ready to bring the right people, the right networks, and the right situations into your life. You just have to activate what God has already put in you!

I believe that in order for us to receive our destiny, our gifts, and our talents, we have to be open to "emerging." The definition of emerging is, *"To move out of or away from something and come into view."* Now, I love that definition and what it says: "to move out of or away from something." Often times that something is us. We are in our own way from emerging or getting to the next level; we could be, at times, our own worst enemies. We believe the doubts and the limits we put on ourselves. We can believe that there is nothing more out of life than what it is right now, and we have very little power to change it. Our vision is blurred by our circumstances at present; we walk in and out of our 24 hour days with no zest or joy for living or hope about what is to come.

But when a mind shift happens and you are ready to emerge and "come into view" with Gods plan, then you will truly see what he has in store for you all along. So, let's embrace emerging, change, growth, and opportunity. We all have 365 days in the year and the same time to live it, why not work on emerging into your being, the reason why you were put on this earth? Do not let the enemy defeat you and fill your head with the lies that you can't or won't activate your blessings. Let the Holy Spirit guide you. Listen to that gentle whisper in your soul that is guiding you to your next chapter—an abundant blessing is about to transpire! So, dream big! Dream so big that those visions and goals you want to achieve for your life are actually quite scary. It's OK to feel the fear—that's when you know you are on the right track.

Chapter 10

WHAT I KNOW FOR CERTAIN.

"Let your faith be bigger than your fear."

~ Author Unknown

There are a lot of things in life that still remain a mystery to me as I am, and forever will be, a student in the class of life. But, there are some truths that I do know that I didn't know before. I know these are true for me because I have lived them thus far throughout my life. So here are a few things I do know for certain.

1. God is with you through the stormy season.

No one has a perfect life; our lives can sometimes look like scenes from a soap opera! Believe me, mine has. But I do know that the storms don't last forever; they are temporary strong fierce winds showing up in our lives to test us, strengthen us and motivate us to keep our faith alive. We don't see that while we are going through it. But if I did not go through the most difficult times in my life, I wouldn't be here today sharing my journey with all of you. It's not easy going through those storms, but God's word says, *"If you have faith as small as a mustard seed"* (**Luke 17-6**): you will see his hand on your life.

Some storms literally knock the wind out of your sails. "A skillful sailor was never taught by a smooth sea." (Author unknown). When you think about your storms and what you went through, and perhaps what you are going through right now, God is ever present. He never said we wouldn't have rainy seasons, but he said he will never leave us in our time of need and never forsake us.

I have had many times in my life when I felt like I was done—I quit and wanted to throw in the towel! But God showed up for me, just when I thought of giving up he showed up and that's what he does for his children: he shows up. Keep the faith. As I am writing this book to you, I am writing to myself to keep the faith alive! I am here to tell you through my life lenses to hold on and stay grounded in God's word over your life for prosperity, joy, abundance, love, and hope. There are things about our lives that we will never know or get the answers to, but in his word he says, *"God is not a man that he should lie"* (**Numbers 23:19**). A blessed life is yours for the taking. Your rainbow after the storm is near.

2. Fail Forward

I must admit that I have an issue: I hate to fail, and when I do fail at a goal or a task that I set out to achieve, I get discouraged. When all the positive self-talk and all of the plans to achieve a goal fails, I can sometimes be like, *"Gosh, what a waste of time!"* I prepared myself and planed all this time to fail!

But today, I have a new insight on failure. Failing at a task you set out to do does not give you the Ok to stop and never try anything new. God isn't giving up on you, so why do you think you have the permission to give up on you? Perhaps failing at a goal or a task is all part of God's plan for you—to learn these lessons so you are ready, equipped, and prepared when the goal you set out for yourself is actually achieved.

I have to remind myself of this daily to keep going, keep walking in his faith, and keep failing forward. You will never know what's in store for you if you keep giving up at every chance you get. Pushing through failure is character building and you will never be getting any further with your goals if you have a *"I'm giving up. Woe is me"* attitude! So, for example, if your goal is to lose some pounds and you are working on your eating habits and fitness, keep at it.

Don't throw in the towel because you have indulged in a weekend of desserts and treats Don't say, *"Oh well, look what I did this weekend; there is no way I can keep up with this healthier habit."* That is a lie you can and you will, stay the course and you push through! Let's say you are in college and you are struggling to keep up with your classes, you may have even failed a class. Don't throw in the towel and say... *"See, I knew it! I'm not cut out for college. I'm going to drop out."* No!

There is no time for that get back on the saddle! If you have to do summer school or night school, you do it! Push through the failing mentality; if you decide to push through these moments, only then you will see God's hand in your life and what blessings he has in store for you. It is bigger than you could ever imagine! When I think of some women who have pushed through all the odds, and have inspired me to keep pursuing my dreams, I think of one remarkable young lady Bethany Hamilton. I recently read about her story and saw her motion picture film about her incredible journey to persevere through major obstacles.

Bethany Hamilton has become a source of inspiration to millions through her story of determination, faith, and hope. At the age of 13, Bethany lost her left arm to a 14-foot tiger shark, which seemed to end her career as a rising surf star. One month after the attack, Bethany returned to the water and within two years had won her first national title. In 2007, she realized her dream of surfing professionally, and, since then, her story has been told in a New York Times bestselling autobiography and in the 2011 film, Soul Surfer. Bethany is involved in numerous charitable efforts, including her own foundation, Friends of Bethany, which reaches out to amputees and youth, encouraging a broken world by offering hope to overcome through Jesus Christ.

Using her platform as a professional athlete to promote living a fit and healthy lifestyle, she authored the book Body and Soul in 2014. Bethany's latest project, Surfs like a Girl, a surf film which will showcase her as one of the best female surfers in the world, is set to release in Spring 2017. (cited www.bethannyhamilton.com).

What a story of encouragement! I mean, talk about never giving up. She could have easily given up when her arm was bitten off by a shark. She could have become bitter and disheartened that this shark took away her ability to surf. But she didn't. She dug deep, picked herself up from her setback, brushed herself off, and moved forward. Through her testimony she has inspired millions all over the world to stand tall in the face of adversity. She never gave up on herself; God was ever present in her life and revealed huge blessings because of what she pushed through and endured. With her missions she is helping others live out their callings.

As I am saying all this to you, I am talking to myself as well! Many times I wanted to give up on this journey of writing and becoming an author, but I stuck it out. Many, many, many times I wanted to stop writing my story and many times I did. I said to myself this task God has put in my heart and assigned me to do is too big and I can't do this. But as I mentioned in previous chapters, God had bigger plans for me, just like he had for Bethany Hamilton and just like he has for you.

So with the Holy Spirit living with in me and refueling my tank, a part of my mission is complete. Romans 5:3-5 says, *"More than that, we rejoice in our sufferings, knowing that suffering produces endurance, and endurance produces character, and character produces hope, and hope does not put us to shame, because God's love has been poured into our hearts through the Holy Spirit who has been given to us."* The journey has been almost four years in the making! God is good. And his guidance helped me push through and never give up on my vision, so don't give up on yours!

3. Love Prevails

I can't say enough about how God loves us, his children. When I felt no love from my past experiences, I came to know God's love for me. I was looking for love in all the wrong places: in friends, family, men, and materialistic things. It left me empty and nothing could fill the void until I came to know my creator personally—above all and everything he loves me unconditionally. When you don't feel the love from society, friends or family, know this truth and know it for certain: you are loved by the one who made you and created you—that I know is true.

What I know for certain is life can be hard, it can be daunting at times but I do know for certain if we keep the faith there is a whole lot of good that can come from it.

I want to share with you a story about a woman, who despite her difficult start in life—which was full of trauma and heartache—she has been blessed and is having a great finish to her life. This woman grew up in a home where she was sexually, verbally, and emotionally abused by her father and the abuse continued until she was 18. While growing up, she felt ashamed, lonely and afraid. She did not know what was in store for her life, and, at the time, she thought that it would never end. Flash forwards years later; this woman is Joyce Meyer and she leads one of the most influential ministries in the world. She has written countless books (one of my favorites is The battlefield of the mind) and is a world renowned motivational speaker who brings her testimony to the world (cited **www.joycemeyer.org**).

Through her journey of brokenness, heartache, and pain, she has come out on top. She is claiming we are victors! I'm sure Joyce Meyer couldn't have dreamed this for her life all those years ago, but God had a bigger plan for her. God knew he was going to turn what was meant to destroy her into good to bless others with her life. Today, Joyce Meyer does just that, and through her testimony, I too can share and write my journey. Am I saying that God has in store for all of us to be Joyce Meyer? No. But, what I am saying to you is that you are not your past. "You may not have had a great start but you are going to have a great finish"-Joyce Meyer. I am a firm believer in that phrase, don't look back, look forward—good things are ahead. I couldn't have even imagined that this was going to be a part of my finish, being an author, breaking the silence, and becoming unashamed.

Restoration is coming; your broken pieces are going to be someone's blessing, someone's inspiration, and someone's encouragement. Let's not be silent with our lives; let your testimony be heard. I want to encourage you to take one step to restoration, then the next, and the next, and so on. It is possible for you to finish GREAT! The odds may be against you and statistically you shouldn't make it, you shouldn't be here, but you are! So live, live like you have never lived before, dare like you have never dared before and above all things love like you have never loved before. God is the great finisher! The great author, how will your story end? I think I know: **GREATLY with his grace!**

Sherika Powell
- AUTHOR -

From being silenced for so long, **Sherika Powell** has now found her voice! She is a woman unchained and on a purpose-driven journey! From 'victim' to 'survivor'... and now a thriver! Her mission is to encourage other women that they too can find their voice and rise through any adversity.

Sherika Powell not only has a heart for women empowerment, and helping women pursue their passions; she is also a childhood survivor of sexual abuse. Her mission is to break the silence from this epidemic that continues to plague our society worldwide. Sherika believes that we should never be ashamed of our broken pieces in our journey because it's in those broken pieces that God's light shines through. All of our stories, our struggles, and our heartaches can be used to uplift and inspire one another. We are all capable of being victors in our everyday lives.

Sherika's many platforms consist of creating and hosting her Women Unchained Podcast Show, Motivational Speaking, Author, Writer as well as her latest platform as the Rogers TV Talk Show Host of "Women on the Rise," a show that highlights women in Durham region, Ontario that are making their mark on the world and pursuing their destiny. Sherika is also a recipient of the CIBWE award for the Top 100 Black Women to Watch in Canada 2016.

She is dedicated to help women everywhere break their silence, pursue their divine calling and become women unchained. With God on our side nothing is impossible!

When Sherika is not speaking, or hosting, she is spending time with her husband, sons, family and girlfriends! Sherika is also an adventure seeker, loves to travel, loves good conversations, dinner parties, reading anything inspirational and can't seem to kick her Starbucks habit!

For more on **Sherika Powell** visit **www.sherikapowell.com**

Social Media Network Of over 3,000 followers

Featured on Radio, TV and womens blogs

DARE TO BE BOLD!

SHERIKA POWELL SPEAKS

Sherika Powell is a dynamic motivational speaker whose passion is igniting the flame in women to achieve their purpose and passions in life. Sherika encourages women everywhere that not only can they become survivors through any adversity they may face but they can also thrive and reach their goals!

Background

Past Events

More about Sherika Powell

Over 13 years of experience working in the field of **social services**. Several years of experience motivating clients to reach their goals.

Women's Retreats
Women's Conferences
Youth Conferences
Panel Discussions
MC/Hosting
Workshop Facilitator

Rogers TV Talk Show Host of **"Women on the Rise"**
Creator of Podcast Show **Women Unchained** Radio
Author of **"A Woman Unchained"** Breaking the silence of childhood sexual abuse.
A Warriors Journey! TBR Summer 2016

Let's Connect!

For more information on booking Sherika Powell as a speaker please contact her via email:

info@sherikapowell.com and website www.sherikapowell.com

If you feel there is a child in danger of abuse, please go to **www.oacas.org** for more information on how to report it.

PUBLISHING

Publishing with
Soul, Creativity & Love

Meraki House Publishing, founded in 2015 has established its brand as an independent virtual publishing house designed to suit your needs as the Author, delivering the highest quality design, writing and editorial, publishing and marketing services to ensure your success.

"Where your needs as an Author have become ours as an independent Publishing House."

WWW.MERAKIHOUSE.COM

In partnership with
www.designisreborn.com

Marnie Kay, Founder & CEO
marniekay.com

CPSIA information can be obtained
at www.ICGtesting.com
Printed in the USA
LVOW04s0816091016
507888LV00020B/123/P